SIMPLE AMISH GARDENING

Publications International, Ltd.

Mary, Mary…How Does Your Garden Grow?

ᘰᘺᓏ

You might wonder: How is Amish gardening different from any other type of gardening? Is a claim of having an Amish garden akin to claiming that you drink Amish water or have Amish cows? In some sense, it's true that good old-fashioned gardening looks similar no matter who does it. But it is equally true that habit and culture influence everything a person does. Thus, in these pages you will find that the Amish have some unique gardening practices that have been handed down for generations and are still in use today.

On the other hand, it is nearly impossible in today's world for a group of people to live in complete isolation. As a result, the Amish have also adopted many widely used methods for gardening that are found in the wider American culture. Besides being traditional, the Amish are also a practical people. If they hear about a particular method or product that works, they will not hesitate to use it. Some have even earned the title of "green Amish" because of the popular organic movement.

So whether you're interested in how the Amish tend to their gardens or just want straightforward gardening advice, this book will inspire you to roll up your sleeves, hum a tune, and go dig in the dirt—just as my Amish mother did for as long as she could swing her hoe.

Planning and Preparing Your Garden

In this chapter, we'll explore the factors you need to consider before you plant anything, including size, location, purpose, and soil testing. We'll also discuss the tools you'll need, when and how to dig, and how to prepare the soil so that your plants have the best chance at living long, prosperous lives.

Look Before You Leap

If you're a beginner or you haven't gardened in a while, there are several factors to consider before the weather turns warm—even while the snow is still falling.

Size It Up

Take into account the amount of space you have available as well as your time and energy resources. Also consider creating a defined border around your garden. You may even choose to divide your garden with internal paths as many Amish do with their kitchen gardens. The paths may be made of sawdust or wood chips and outlined with boards that form raised garden beds. Paths could also be cement walkways that are raised above the planting area.

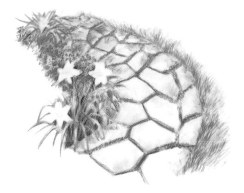

Some Amish families use bricks to make striking borders around their gardens. Railroad ties or old barn beams can also be used to define the space and make slightly raised beds.

Paths allow you to enter the garden to pull vegetables or weeds after it's rained without getting your feet muddy. Picket, board, or wire fences are often used to enclose gardens that have walkways.

Location, Location, Location

Most vegetables prefer a sunny location, however some items, such as lettuce, prefer not to have full sunlight all day. Thus, a garden that gets partial sun and partial shade at different times of the day may still be effective. Having a water source nearby is an essential factor to consider when planning your garden. And you'll find that a kitchen garden is more convenient if it is located near the house, so you can quickly go out and pick fruits and vegetables for your meals.

Plant with a Purpose

The purpose of your garden will determine what you'll plant. Do you want to grow your own flowers for a family wedding? Do you just want to eat your fill of healthy vegetables? The Amish plant lots of red beets and cucumbers to serve at Sunday dinners after church.

Test, Don't Guess

If you plan to do all the work to dig and plant a garden, you'll want to make sure that those little seeds and plants have their best shot at growing. To increase the likelihood of success, consider having your soil tested:

✿ Call your local Cooperative Extension service, and ask them to come to your home and test your soil (at little or no cost), or purchase a kit to do it yourself. Soil-testing kits are available at most hardware stores. Be sure to follow the directions on the testing kit.

Consider having your soil tested in the fall. Many people do it in the spring, which causes a backlog at the Extension Service office and could delay getting the test results back.

Breaking Ground

After you've had the soil tested and planned your garden, you'll be ready to dig into the soil. Knowing how to treat the soil is an important aspect of successful gardening.

Working Up the Soil

There are several ways to prepare the soil for planting. Many Amish people dig up their kitchen gardens by hand with a shovel. After digging one length, add a layer of manure, then lay the dirt back over the manure. Treating the soil with such care year after year results in fertile soil and heavy yields.

Depending on church regulations, some Amish folks use hand tillers to work up their gardens. You may find it helpful to leave one end of the garden open—without a border—so that you can easily enter with a tiller.

To do a thorough job of working the soil, you should first till the soil in one direction and then go back over it crosswise.

If you have a rather large garden, using a horse to plow up and till is much better for the soil than using a tractor because the soil is not packed down excessively by the weight and rotation of the tires.

Know Your Soil

Sandy soil tends to be looser and will run through your fingers like sand at the beach. It is generally ready for planting earlier in the spring. Clay soil is dense and sticks together more because it retains more moisture. Clay soil takes longer to dry off in the spring and will also need more compost every season so that it's easier to work up and till.

If your area tends to have excessive rain in the spring, consider preparing raised beds or hilled-up rows in the fall. This will allow some water to drain off so you can plant sooner.

Enriching the Soil

When turning over the soil in their gardens, the Amish add fertilizer at the same time. Those who have farms (or know farmers) always have an ample supply of horse, cow, or chicken manure on hand. Consider these options:

�☞ Purchase composted manure from farmers in your area.

�☞ See if you can get free compost from city services. Some towns collect leaves and grass clippings which decompose over the winter. Adding such compost to your garden in the spring will considerably loosen up clay soil.

�☞ Make your own compost with scraps from the kitchen, leaves and grass clippings from your lawn, and manure. Mix these items, let them become compost, and spread it on the garden the following spring.

Depending on the conditions, it could take a few weeks to a few months for this mixture to become compost. If the mixture is put in a composting barrel in the sunshine and is turned daily, then it will only take a few weeks until the compost is ready to use. If the mixture is stirred once a week, it will take about 3–4 months, and if it just sits in a pile, it will need to sit throughout the fall and winter.

Chicken manure can be very potent. Spread a thin layer of it on the ground a week or so before working it into the soil. This will allow the rain to leech (dilute) it somewhat before planting. If there's no rain, spray it with a hose to dilute it. Otherwise, it may kill the plants or make them unhealthy.

Planting, Transplanting, and Propagating

In this chapter, we'll discuss various aspects of the planting process, including the ease of growing certain plants, the best time to plant, and types of propagation. Flowers and their place in the Amish woman's garden will also be discussed.

The Two Commandments

There are two rules of thumb that every gardener should follow: rotate your crops and give plants room to grow.

Rotate Crops

If you're planting in a garden that was used the previous year, be sure to rotate your crops. Different types of plants take different kinds of nutrients from the soil, so if you plant the same thing in the same place every year, you'll stress both the soil and your plants.

Don't Crowd Your Plants

Like humans, plants need elbow room...with some exceptions. For instance, peas generally prefer lots of company. Simply follow the directions on the seed packets or ask the person from whom you purchased

Helpful Hint

Each year, draw a diagram of your garden so you don't forget what you planted (and where) the previous year.

the seedlings how far apart to space them. Some guidelines are also noted below.

Vegetables

> ꩜
>
> Mark off inches and feet on the handle of your hoe so that you don't need to carry a measuring stick.

These days, health-conscious consumers want to grow tasty vegetables that are free of harsh chemicals and pesticides. Fortunately, the Amish have been "green" (i.e., practicing organic gardening) for centuries.

Ease of Growth

Some plants are much more likely to give you success than others. Many beans, for example, are very forgiving of soil type and a beginning gardener's lack of expertise. Eggplant is another story. Avoid it if you're a novice gardener. When you peruse seed catalogs (see Appendix for suggestions), pay attention to the codes that clarify the disease resistance, hardiness, and other features related to the product.

Also pay attention to growing zones, which are related to weather and frost dates. These zones, along with the plants' descriptions, will give you a good idea as to a product's fussiness or ease of growth.

A Time for Everything

As the Bible states, "To every thing there is a season, and a time to every purpose under the heaven . . ." (Ecclesiastes 3:1), and planting your garden is no exception. Here are some guidelines on when to plant some common vegetables.

When to Plant	What to Plant
Very early (as soon as the soil can be prepared)	Asparagus roots, broccoli, cabbage, chard, endive, kale, lettuce, onion sets (bulbs), peas, radishes, spinach
Early (1–2 weeks before the average date of the last spring frost)	Cauliflower, Chinese cabbage, potatoes
Soon after the last spring frost	Beets, carrots, celery, hardy varieties of early corn and snap beans
About 2–3 weeks after the average date of the last spring frost	Corn (mid- or late-season), cucumbers, lima beans, melons, peppers, squash, sweet potatoes, tomatoes
About 2 months before the average date of the first fall frost (for fall crops)	Broccoli and other plants in the cabbage family, garlic, lettuce, peas, spinach

Direct Seeding

Vegetables that are best suited for direct seeding into the garden without first starting them indoors include: beans of all kinds, beets, carrots, corn, kale and other greens, lettuce, onion sets, peas, radishes, and spinach. Follow packet directions for location, timing, and spacing of seeds.

Plant fine seeds, such as salad greens, and root crops, such as carrots and beets, in the garden's better, more fertile soil. Plant beans in the part of the garden that's lumpy and less fertile. Squash and cucumbers do not demand the best soil, but they will appreciate it.

Squash and cucumbers do not take long to emerge after the weather warms up, so they can be planted directly into hills, which keep the roots from becoming waterlogged if wet weather or clay soil is an issue. Melons also thrive in hills.

Helpful Hint

If you set plants out early, place plastic milk jugs with their bottoms cut out (and the cap off) over seedlings to protect them against frost. The jugs act like mini greenhouses.

Making a Hill

Dig a depression several inches deep and about two feet wide. In this hole, drop a good shovel full of manure. Cover this with soil and build up a rounded hill of about 5 or 6 inches. Smooth out the very top and lay 4 or 5 seeds in a circle around the top. Poke them into the ground about an inch or so. Put a thin layer of compost or mulch over the soil to keep it moist. Seedlings should emerge within a week or two.

Transplanting

In the old days, the Amish would start almost all of their plants in their homes or in cold frames. However, the times they are a-changing. Many Amish folks purchase seedlings from greenhouses, which have become viable businesses for some Amish families.

Starting Plants from Seeds

If you'd like to grow your own plants indoors to save money or just for fun, here's how to do it:

1. Use a clean, relatively flat container with a clear plastic lid. Fill it half to one-third full of sterile seed-starter (moist, not soggy).
2. Plant the seeds and label the container.
3. Place it in indirect sunlight and wait for the seeds to emerge.

☞ Transplant individual tomato and pepper plants into cell packs or small yogurt containers to give them time to grow larger before planting them in the garden.

☞ Acclimate plants by putting them in a cool (but protected) place for several days before planting them in the garden.

☞ Transplant seedlings into the garden in the evening or on a cloudy day so that the sun doesn't bake the fragile plants before they get used to their new environment.

Recycle Leftover Seeds

Many seeds will last for 4 or 5 years if kept in a cool, dry place like a glass jar in the freezer. Sweet corn should not be kept more than a year to ensure the best germination, but beans, carrots, peas, and peppers will last for up to 3 years.

ᴄʀᴇ Water transplanted seedlings when you put them into the ground, and if it doesn't rain, water them daily until they get a good start.

Neither Seed Nor Seedling

Many vegetables are not born of seeds or seedlings. These include bulbs, root vegetables, and celery.

Onions

The onions that you use for salads (such as green onions), cooking, or storing over winter are usually bought in bulbs (onion sets). To plant, use a hoe to mark out a furrow about 5–6 inches deep. Then place the bulbs in the soft dirt about 2 inches deep on either side of the furrow, so they're about 4 inches apart in a zigzag fashion.

Sweet onions, such as Vidalia and Walla Walla, are bought in bundles and are planted in the same fashion as other onions, except that the tops should stick out of the ground.

Potatoes

You can buy certified seed potatoes at a hardware store, but the Amish usually make their own because home-raised potatoes simply taste better than store-bought ones. Using leftover potatoes from one year:

1. Cut the seed potatoes into pieces, making sure you have an eye (a little bump or indenture) in each piece.
2. Let these pieces sit in a bucket for 4 or 5 days.
3. Dig a furrow 3–4 inches deep. Place the potato pieces firmly into the row about 10 inches apart and cover.

4. As the potatoes grow, hill them up by hoeing more dirt up around them.

Sweet Potatoes

Although sweet potato plants can be ordered from a catalog or purchased at a greenhouse, it's easy to grow your own:

1. In February—using a sweet potato from last year's garden (or a clean store-bought one)—stick 4 toothpicks into the sides about two-thirds of the way down, and anchor the potato in a wide-mouth quart jar full of water.
2. Place the jar and sweet potato near a window that gets sun, and keep it filled with water. Within several weeks, small plants should start growing out of the potato.
3. After these plants have grown to about 5 or 6 inches long, snap them off at the base, and stick the seedlings in water to grow roots. It shouldn't take long. New plants will keep growing for some weeks.
4. As soon as the plants have roots, plant them into hills. Sweet potatoes like heat and grow well in warm weather.

Celery

While growing your own celery is not an easy task, it is an old Amish custom. And at Amish weddings, it's a tradition to place celery hearts in glass vases to decorate the dinner tables. Sweet-and-sour celery is also a staple at Amish wedding feasts.

1. After the last spring frost, dig a trench as wide as a garden shovel, but only half as deep.
2. Shake a thin layer of chicken manure into the trench.
3. Soak the trench before placing the plants, then keep it

soaked with water for a week so that the young transplants don't get burned.

4. The celery plants should be about 4–6 inches tall when placed into the trench. As the plants grow, hill up more dirt around them (but don't cover the leaves). This will blanch the lower part of the plants. (You can also put a paper bag over the stalks to blanch them.) By November, which is the traditional Amish wedding season, the plants will be mature.

Sweet-and-Sour Creamed Celery

Cook 4 cups chopped celery with ½ cup water just until tender. Add ½ cup sugar. Combine 1 tablespoon flour and ¼ cup water to make a smooth paste. Add ½ teaspoon salt and ½ cup cream to the paste and stir into the hot celery. Add 1 tablespoon butter and 2 tablespoons vinegar to the celery. Stir, and bring to a boil to thicken.

Treasured Fruits

Most Amish gardens have some type of berries, as well as ground cherries, rhubarb plants, and a grape arbor.

Strawberries

Strawberries are the most common type of fruit that the Amish grow. They come in two kinds—June bearers and everbearers—so be sure to buy the type that's suitable for your climate. They generally like rich soil that has been

supplemented with 2–4 inches of
compost several months before
they're planted in early spring.
During the plants' initial summer,
pick off blossoms and cut off run-
ners to strengthen the plants. If
they are planted in fall, this is not
necessary.

Raspberries and Blackberries

Most Amish gardeners grow raspberries and blackberries.
In early spring, place young plants about 3 feet apart in soil
that is well drained and has been fertilized with composted
manure.

Ground Cherries

Ground cherries are an essential part of many Amish
gardens, particularly in Pennsylvania. The fruit grows inside
a paperlike shell and is ripe when the cherry turns yellow.
It has a sweet flavor that tastes similar to pineapple.

Grapes

Rare is the Amish garden that does not have a grape arbor.
Grapes are propagated from roots and should be planted in
well-drained, fertile soil. Immediately after planting, cut the
plants back to a single cane with 2 strong buds. During the
plants' first summer, train the young vine up a 5-foot stake
set beside it and remove the weakest of the two vines. In the
spring of the second season, prune the vine and train it to
climb up and over a 7-foot arbor.

Rhubarb

Rhubarb is used for pies and rhubarb sauce and is propagated from roots or by transplanting from someone else's garden in the early spring. The plants will produce vigorous stalks throughout the spring and early summer if you cover the roots heavily with a mixture of straw and manure in February or March.

Flowers

Flowers are the expression of an Amish woman's soul. She can freely decide what types to plant, just for the joy and aesthetic pleasure that flowers provide. When you drive through Amish country in the summertime, you'll see evidence of the love of bright, beautiful, blooming things.

An Amish garden will often be bordered with a row of bright and lovely petunias or marigolds. You might also see long-stemmed gladiolus, asters, cockscombs, snapdragons, and zinnias as well as daisies, irises, lilacs, and peonies.

The Wild Side

While most people see no value in dandelions, some Amish folks pick them and use them to make a warm salad or wine, which can also be used to ease a persistent cough.

Nurturing and Protecting Your Plants

༄ळ༖ण

This chapter will discuss how to take care of your garden throughout the summer growing season so that you can expect a bountiful harvest. Aspects of care include watering, feeding, weeding, and mulching, as well as simple ways to protect your garden from various diseases, pests, and weather factors.

A Drink of Water

Keeping young plants watered is one of the most important ways to get them off to a good start. In early spring, the seedlings that you plant (cabbage family and other greens) will generally not need to be watered often, as Mother Nature will take care of it. However, vegetables that are planted later in the season, such as tomatoes, peppers, and sweet potatoes, may need more watering to get them started.

In mid-summer, a garden should receive about an inch of water per week. Never use watering cans or sprinklers to water plants in the heat of the day because the water evaporates too quickly. Soaker hoses can be used any time of day because the water goes directly to the roots.

Feeding Plants

Over the years, the Amish have perfected homemade plant food recipes for specific types of fruits and vegetables. Here are some of the most common:

☙ **Broccoli, cabbage, and cauliflower:** Dissolve ¾ cup salt in 1 gallon of water. When the plants begin to form heads, spray them with this mixture twice a week to help them grow larger.

☙ **Berries and grapes:** Mix together 1 gallon of wood ash, 1 gallon of hydrated lime, and a handful of sulfur. Sprinkle on and around each berry plant once a month during February, March, and April, and once again when small berries appear on the vines. This will make the plants stronger and encourage them to bear more fruit.

☙ **Tomatoes:** Add 1 teaspoon of Epsom salts to each plant at the time of planting. Dissolve 2 tablespoons of Epsom salt in 1 gallon of water and give your tomato plants a drink of this every week while they're blooming to increase yield and prevent blight.

☙ **For general house and garden plants:** Mix 1 teaspoon each of saltpeter, ammonia, cream of tartar, and Epsom salts in 1 gallon of water. Store in a glass jug and water plants with this mixture once a month for healthier plants.

Beat the Weeds

No Amish woman would like to be caught with weeds in her garden. A weed-free garden is a source of pride for the Amish as it shows their love of order and discipline. Weeds take moisture, light, and nutrients away from plants, so weed your garden at least once a week.

☙ Begin weeding early in the season just after weeds sprout.

On sunny days, hoe early in the morning so that the sun will kill the weeds later in the day. Also, you're less likely to get a sunburn (and skin cancer) if you go out early.

If the soil is wet, don't put your pulled weeds back in the garden—they might take root again. Instead, collect them in a bucket and dispose of them elsewhere.

Mulching between rows and around plants helps to control weeds, conserve water, and prevent fruit from rotting.

The Amish commonly use straw, maple leaves, old sawdust (not fresh), pine needles, and composted or strawy manure for mulch. Newspapers weighed down with grass clippings also make a good mulch.

Controlling Predators

The Amish have a number of simple ways to protect plants from destructive insects, worms, and animals:

Bean and potato beetles: Dust plants with hydrated lime as soon as they emerge, and reapply after it rains.

Cabbage worms: Dust cabbage plants with a mixture of 1 quart flour and 2 teaspoons baking soda while the dew is still on the plants. You may also sprinkle them with baby powder. Repeat dustings after it rains.

Carrot, radish, and beet worms: To repel worms, sprinkle wood ash into the row before planting seeds.

Corn borer: When corn is starting to show silk at the tips of the ears, dab a bit of mineral oil on the silks to deter bugs.

Cucumber, melon, and squash bugs: Dissolve 1 tablespoon saltpeter in a 2-gallon pail of water. Add one pint of this to the soil when you plant.

Besides using dusts and sprays—either homemade or store-bought—the Amish use other methods to protect their plants. Here are a few tried-and-true tricks of the trade:

 Cover plants with white permeable floating row covers.

 Plant vegetables near odorous plants (such as marigolds, dill, onions, garlic, etc.) that will repel bugs and animals.

 Place pieces of highly scented soap, such as Dial or Irish Spring, among garden plants to keep deer away.

 Attract helpful insects to the garden by planting flowers among the vegetables. For example, ladybugs eat their weight in aphids daily, and praying mantises eat lots of mosquitoes.

 Plant castor beans at the ends of rows of sweet potatoes to prevent moles from attacking the tubers.

 The Amish also erect birdhouses to attract purple martins to their gardens. These birds eat insects such as grasshoppers, flies, Japanese beetles, stink bugs, moths, and flying ants.

Weather Factors

Mother Nature can be unpredictable. However, the Amish are resourceful and use some simple methods to deal with issues such as frost, drought, heat, and over-abundance of rain.

ᴄᴿᴇ To protect plants (such as those in the cabbage family) from frost, cover them with plastic jugs with the bottoms cut out. Cover blooming strawberries with old bed sheets or floating row covers.

ᴄᴿᴇ To conserve water, especially during a drought, the Amish use whatever is available to water their plants, including used dishwater, water used in cooking (such as water used to hard-boil eggs), or water from a rain barrel or a wringer washer.

ᴄᴿᴇ During times of extreme heat, keep plants well watered, but remember to water them in the evening. Also, construct some kind of shading (for example, wide boards propped up by bricks) to place over lettuce and other greens while still allowing for air movement around the base of the plants.

ᴄᴿᴇ If you have to go into the garden to harvest after it's been raining, wait until the plants have dried off to avoid blight, especially of beans. Also, lay a board on the area where you need to step to prevent the soil from becoming packed down.

In the absence of television, radio, and the Internet, *Raber's New American Almanac* offers important weather information that assists the Amish in making gardening decisions.

Harvesting and Storing

ᘑᘥᙁᘚ

This chapter focuses on how and when to harvest various crops, and how to preserve them for future use. In addition, we'll also address how to prepare your garden for the winter.

Leaves of Green

Greens such as lettuce, spinach, chard, and kale are generally eaten fresh, so you can harvest them at any time.

ᑕᑎ Using a knife, cut off lettuce and kale several inches above the root. They will keep producing as long as the weather is cool enough and you keep them watered.

ᑕᑎ You can also pick off individual spinach and chard leaves. The plants will continue to produce and the smaller leaves will keep growing. Spinach usually has a shorter growing season compared to chard. Chard can last all summer and even until the first frost if watered during hot, dry spells. Chard leaves taste better the more mature they are.

Extending the Season

Most green leafy vegetables can be sown in early August, but they can grow almost year round if you live in a warmer climate. You might also construct a cold frame to grow greens over winter.

A simple cold frame can be made by placing bales of straw around the area where you plan to grow winter greens. In November, plant spinach, lettuce, or corn mâche (corn salad) inside this insulated frame. Water it and place some salvaged windowpanes or clear plastic on top of it. By early spring, you should have nice salad greens that are ready to eat.

෴ Because corn mâche does not attract snails, it is one of the best choices for growing in a cold frame.

Vegetables with Pods

Some vegetables with pods are usually harvested in the green stage, while others are normally left to dry on the vine before they are harvested.

Peas

Most Amish folks love their peas. With some varieties, the whole pod can be eaten raw or cooked. But the shell type is the most common for eating and preserving.

Peas must be picked when they are ready because they can quickly become overripe. When the pods look fat, open some to check their maturity. Peas picked a bit on the tender side have the best flavor. Peas should be picked every two days.

Lima Beans

Lima beans grow slowly and are usually harvested at the end of summer. If the plants stay healthy, they will bear until frost.

෴ When the pods are fat and well filled, it is time to pick. Lima beans grow more slowly than peas, so they can be picked once a week.

ᴄᴛᴇ Many Amish people can lima beans, but they taste best when processed and frozen.

Green Beans

Green beans can be harvested when they're the size of what you'd typically see in a grocery store. The Amish eat them fresh and also can them for winter enjoyment.

Root Vegetables

M ost root crops, such as beets, carrots, onions, potatoes, sweet potatoes, and turnips, can be stored for winter eating without canning.

Beets

It is time to pull and cook beets when they reach several inches in diameter. Some varieties, such as Lutz, taste best when they are larger.

Don't discard beet tops! They are sweeter than spinach when chopped and cooked briefly (until wilted) with just a bit of water and salt.

Carrots

If covered with a nice layer of leaves, carrots can be left in the garden all winter and dug up as needed.

Onions

When their leaves fold over and turn brown, onions are ready to pull. Spread them out in a shady place to dry for a week or so. After that, small onions can be braided together and hung up for later use. Snip the leaves off larger onions and place them in mesh bags.

Potatoes

When the blossoms appear on a potato plant, dig around the edge of the plant for "new" potatoes. Do not dig up the whole plant.

"Onion skins very thin, mild the winter coming in. Onion skins thick and tough, coming winter cold and rough."

—**Amish Proverb**

Whole plants should be harvested in dry weather about 2–3 weeks after the plant dies. Dry the potatoes in a warm but shady place for 2–3 hours before storing them in a cool (about 40–45 degrees), dark place.

Sweet Potatoes

Sweet potatoes should be harvested just before, or immediately after, the first frost. Their skins are tender, so handle them with care.

Spread sweet potatoes out on newspaper to dry in a warm place (about 80 degrees) for about 2 weeks. Then, store in a cool (50 degrees), dry place for the fall and winter.

Turnips

Turnips can be left in the garden until early fall; they actually become sweeter in cool weather. When you're ready to harvest, simply pull them up by their tops.

Neither Pod nor Root

Other vegetables and some fruits can also be preserved for the winter. Canned goods keep best in a cool dark place, such as a basement.

Cabbage

Cabbage is ready to harvest whenever it has formed a nice large head, but that will depend on the type and whether it was planted in early spring or late summer.

Winter Squash

Winter squash, such as butternut, hubbard, and buttercup, should be left on the vine until their skins are extremely hard, which is usually in late summer or early fall. To harvest, cut them from the vine, leaving a 2–3 inch stem on each squash. Let them cure in the sun for a week or more, then store in a cool, dry place for winter.

Fruits

The Amish can most of their fruits, including berries, peaches, plums, cherries, and pears. Some Amish families can up to 1,000 quarts of fruits and vegetables each year! The Amish also freeze some fruits and make them into jams.

Blackberries, Raspberries, and Blueberries

To can blackberries, raspberries, and blueberries, simply fill jars with fresh berries, add ½ cup sugar, and pour in enough water to cover the berries, leaving an inch of room at the top. Tighten lids and submerge in boiling water for 20 minutes. Blueberries can also be frozen, but this should be done without washing and without sugar. Washing makes them tough. They can be washed before they're eaten.

Strawberries

Amish families with gas freezers preserve strawberries whole without sugar, or crushed with some sugar. Strawberries are usually not canned except when made into jam.

Preparing Your Garden for Winter

When Jack Frost comes for a visit, most of your gardening will already be done for the season. However, you can begin winterizing some parts of your garden before then:

☙ Harvest any remaining aboveground vegetables.

☙ Pull out all dead plants and grind them for compost (or throw them away), then work up the ground with a tiller.

☙ Scatter crimson clover or rye seed over the ground, till the dirt and seed together, and let them cover the garden until spring when you'll work them into the soil and start all over again. Clover, in particular, will loosen and enrich the soil wherever it is planted.

☙ This procedure can be done in stages. For example, when your potatoes come out, you can plant some clover seed in that area, even though the rest of the garden is still producing.

☙ After all this is done, go into the house, make some hot tea, put your feet up, and take a long rest!